DAUGHTER TONGUE
OMOTARA JAMES

This is a work of fiction. All names, characters, places, and incidents are a product of the author's imagination. Any resemblance to real events or persons, living or dead, is entirely coincidental.

Published by Akashic Books

ISBN: 978-1-61775-634-4

Printed in China through Four Colour Print Group, Louisville, Kentucky
First printing

Akashic Books
Brooklyn, New York, USA
Ballydehob, Co. Cork, Ireland
Twitter: @AkashicBooks
Facebook: AkashicBooks
E-mail: info@akashicbooks.com
Website: www.akashicbooks.com

African Poetry Book Fund
Prairie Schooner
University of Nebraska
110 Andrews Hall
Lincoln, Nebraska 68588

TABLE OF CONTENTS

PREFACE
by DéLana R.A. Dameron

To be of many places at once—like British-born American poet Omotara James, who is also the daughter of Nigerian and Trinidadian immigrants—is to hold many selves in one body. To be a poet with such a lineage and home-knowing (or is it unknowing?) is to wrestle with language that is foreign and familiar. It is to be in a constant state of being inside a nation with eyes and blood outside of it. Always reaching, reaching. Possessing at all times many tongues—the blood tongue, the land tongue, and so: the *Daughter Tongue*. Biting and lush. Evolving. It is a different knowing, even dialect, that James must speak in the language of her blood in order to write these poems against and within and beside a tradition (American, Trini, Naija) to comprise a story only her own.

Omotara James's chapbook *Daughter Tongue* tells many stories at once, while concurrently telling a central story: the challenges, triumphs, beauty, and ugliness of a mother-daughter relationship, and the stories of a daughter trying to find words to make the *unsayable* said and heard and seen. In it, we follow a speaker's attempts to reconcile a mother who has her own versions of who the speaker *should* be, while the speaker blossoms into who she is—the whole of her—and who she falls in and out of love with.

In-approaching Omotara James's *Daughter Tongue,* we have "two choices: / to believe nothing / or everything" she writes to us. Choose *everything*.

James's chapbook covers a vast terrain, an impressive feat. *Daughter Tongue* explores the complexities of one who is both trying to love herself and others, even when she herself is multiple selves at once, and also always evolving—even if the exterior, the body, remains what seems a constant burden to the speaker. She asks: "What if the body // is just the throw-away?"

The opening poem "Prologue to a Name" situates us with a daughter who was born into a tradition, by describing how at birth one exists seven days before given a name. There is ceremony in calling out what or who that newborn body would become. James complicates this idea of celebration by opening the poem, and yet, the whole collection with a profound statement: "THE BODY IS AN unmarked grave before it is given a name."

Her poems exist in these unnamed interstices: what is love between two bodies, no matter how the world, or mother, might name it? What is the body to the beholder, no matter how the world, or mother, might name it?

To spend time with this work, with these cracked-open poems, is to resist naming, as the speaker and mother in the poem "After the Feast" so often does:

> mommy is careful not to use the word *breakup*,
> instead:
>
> she might pull at
> the shirt to cover my backside,
> inquire about my plans
> for the day,
>
> suggest I go
> to the gym.
> Insist

or, from "Proverb":

> *cookie,* which we all know
>
> was my first word. Not *Mama.*
> Even when we don't discuss
> gastric bypass
> we do.

James, in these poems, shows us that she is not afraid to show you the interior spaces, *the meat of it.* The complex muddle of it. At times, we stand in the position of the mother, trying to understand, awaiting a name, and James wants us to stand with her in the in-between. This work is evident throughout the collection, but succeeds in a section of the poem "GenderMotherFucker":

Mother

When I told my mother that I was actually in love with Madeline, that she was more than my friend, she asked me if it was love at first sight. I didn't have to think about it. *Yes.* It was a strange question, but I also wondered how she knew, when I couldn't have guessed. But, weren't you *just* in love with a man? *Yes and no, Mom. He was both . . .* I had displeased my mother profoundly: to the point of fascination. Stunned, she gave up on trying to change me and wanted only to understand. Silently, on opposite sides of the island of her seventies-style kitchen, we had come to our first real, adult agreement. I would no longer belong to her, nor she to me.

James is at once daughter, adult, lover, a sexual being; one who is struggling to articulate for a mother who is struggling to understand. The distances between them: we know, through this collection there will always be a figurative and literal ocean. James accomplishes this through a dexterity of form and voice, through looking at the same stories from different angles. This focusing and refocusing allows the reader to understand that it is not often we *deal with the difficult* and then are done.

James's speakers must confront and re-confront their demons. These speakers are confident while also concerned with self-scrutinizing, with truth-telling, with tenderness. They open us to a world we want to return to again and again. Her poems invite us to journey with her to places "where the love is / The Greatest." And we trust her. And we *go.*

PROLOGUE TO A NAME

THE BODY IS AN unmarked grave before it is given a name. On the seventh day the priest, parents, family, elders and the invited gather 'round the newborn in purpose and ceremony. They assemble with the necessary ingredients for life. Place them on her tongue. Bring sugar so that the child might experience some sweetness. Honey: in case the sugar is too sweet she spits. No child rejects the pace of honey. Salt: because there is goodness in all things. Crocodile pepper: so that the woman's life will not be too plain. *Ata ire*: for fertility. Water: for it has no enemy. *Obi* or Kola nut: to ensure the girl will *no iku danu*. One taste and the child will vomit death away. *Orogobo* or bitter kola: so that she may grow ripe with age. Now, the child is ready:

THE TALK

we never had the talk
about the birds or the bees or the boys
who chased me

throbbing, through the hallways at school,
past combination lockers and classrooms

where i sprinted for my life, turning right,
sometimes left, for the atrium, but they
could always find the line to my scent,

an invisible thread, i could feel the vibrations
treads of their soles

scuff 'cross the linoleum
floors of my virginity,
except i didn't know that word then, only

the muscular friction of clumsy hands
over then under the brown sash

of the Brownies uniform
we were made to wear, every Tuesday and Thursday
something about school spirit   used to love to run

to chase the blood in my thighs
—not the boys   they preferred us still

beneath them, swollen with the silence
of seedlings desperate to sprout
as they took turns reaping us,

digging their fingers into our soft, brown flesh
breaking in our brand new breasts

and twisting our nipples (hard)
like they were turning the earth, like it was their rite
to pull us through that passage

breathless
still, I recall the first prod,
the first pinch of my fat in his flat fingers,
the surprise of his nails like ice,
like the first frost or heavy snowfall of memory

when my mother bundled us up
in our voluminous snowsuits

for the inclement weather.
since the forecast called for precipitation and
i was impenetrable to the elements outside

except for my eyes. memory in hindsight
is a stained pair of underwear held up

to the sunlight   now i see
beneath every zipped zipper, tucked mitten
clasped button and tied earflap,

the difference between marching out of the house with something,
versus nothing.

HAIRCUT

/ When I finally tell my mother / I am in love with a woman /
she looks up / from the frying pan and / I look down
as she asks me / what it is that we do / She means,
sexually / She wants / details / She waits / for my response /

I think it's time to invest in coconuts.
/ Never learned / to stomach / the smell / of mother's palm oil /
inside our American seventies kitchen / announcing itself /
in hot / splatters / across / the clean lines / of the cold porcelain /

I still lay / my temple / across a cool surface / splay my troubles /
over a tiled / floor / limbs / like I'm seven again / naked from the waist /
beneath my mother's / steady hand / and long / silver / scissors
/ which always feel / like surprise ice / against my chubby pubis

My eyes / pinned East / beneath her / impatient voice,
I said don't move / My girlhood / open / as the morning
blinds / the light / I wish was brighter / but I
understand my mother / is trying to // protect // me

against the woman / I cannot see / whom the world awaits /
When she's finished / cutting / she dusts the loose hairs / off
like a janitor / underpaid / sighs / and I'm allowed / to be
a girl again / pull up my shorts / and run to play /

Outside / the air / tastes like / honeysuckle / and I
am on the cusp / of forgetting / until she calls /
/ me home / I pretend / not to hear / her questions /
She wants / to know / where I / am going /

A WALL

In the evening, I remind Bruce
to shut the door to the closet,
because the kitten already knows

a door is a wall you cannot climb—
you must walk through.
Yesterday

I promised Jennifer
I was over you,
then logged into

your Instagram,
counted backwards
to the last photo of us

trying on dresses
like I used to
with my mother

who promised to tell the truth,
especially when it wasn't pretty.
One day, I remember

leaving the mall
with a bag full of bras
and grabbing her

hand on the escalator,
resting my head on her shoulder.
I was ten

when she pulled away
saying, *people will
think we're lesbians.*

Sometimes
around 4 AM
my full stomach

growls like the kitten
paws at the door
she can't claw through—

in every house
a room
for the unknown.

MAMA WATA

The saliva seeps from the glands at the base of my tongue
the way the earth rejects the rain after (or worse)—
during the flood. Pursed lips seal in the fluid.

My tongue   womb-ly   like a baby
sinking
further from consciousness back into the amnio.
This
is a warning.

RUFUS, I NEVER MET YOU, BUT I WANT TO TELL YOU

after Larry Levis

this cup
(you can't see it)
could be my brother
(used to have one)
or my sister
(used to be one)

it's empty
but you can still see the ring inside
the height
to which a thing within its walls could rise
before leaking
out the bottom

you have two choices:
to believe nothing
or everything I tell you

did I have a choice
when a stranger
the Bible told me was my brother
picked me up
with a sweet smile and clammy palms
to drink me

tell me *yes* and I'll sing Halleluiah
pick up that cup over here there
(one with the smears' could be my sister)
and smash her

TIDES

On the toilet
I think about my students
who can't agree

           how to *define* gentrification

           only how it feels

           dense / yellow / ochre

s i n k i n g

           like a shofar
           into the throat of the bowl

           waste complicates ritual

           creates layers
           of listening

when Leonard Cohen hums

           you like it darker

           from his starry throne

           earthworms bristle
           in burrows

           stretch to the surface

release anchors

u n d e r g r o u n d

tides

of invertebrate vibrato

THREE WOMEN / TWO TRANSFERS AND A TOKEN / ONE REINCARNATION

(for Max Ritvo)

Lately,
flossing at the sink or
tweezing on the toilet

or hovering over the pregnant woman
I gave my seat to
when I haven't been touched in months;

I stare into my reflection: into my mouth
towards the fleshy back. See life
evaporate into nothing—

a hole where there was *ivory*
once   and I sink like a cavity
into soft tissue, as it is

proof of all we cannot repeat. Collectively,

a woman's baby gurgles
above the engine and the heat. I shift
my eyes. Open my mouth. Make sounds.

GENDERMOTHERFUCKER

Gender

He was average in height, build, weight, but like no other—and I would never have noticed him had I not fallen stupid in love. His love poems were terrible, his breath tasted like smoke, but the day he kissed me changed my identity. Anyone can conjure the image of a dog chasing her own tail, but if you've actually seen it, *O*, the small spectacle creates a kind of joy separate from the humor of life, but just as true. The frenzy of the beast in chase transcends the gifts of meditation and I would have torn my life in half with my own teeth if he had asked me to, though, knowing me, I would have done it anyway.

GENDERMOTHERFUCKER

Mother

When I told my mother that I was actually in love with Madeline, that she was more than my friend, she asked me if it was love at first sight. I didn't have to think about it. *Yes.* It was a strange question, but I also wondered how she knew, when I couldn't have guessed. But, weren't you *just* in love with a man? *Yes and no, Mom. He was both* . . . I had displeased my mother profoundly: to the point of fascination. Stunned, she gave up on trying to change me and wanted only to understand. Silently, on opposite sides of the island of her seventies-style kitchen, we had come to our first real, adult agreement. I would no longer belong to her, nor she to me.

GENDERMOTHERFUCKER

Fucker

He just disappeared. You know, the way people did before the internet. "You remember Larry, Ohhh . . . my first husband. Eh-heh, he went out for milk after dinner one day—" That old trope loses its gums when it happens to you. It was an Impressionist sunrise the moment he turned back to kiss me as if he couldn't *bear* to leave. I thought he was magic, when he was just

the
wand
itself.

I was the fucking magician.

A MOTHER CAN SEE MORE SITTING DOWN THAN A CHILD STANDING UP

(Yoruba Proverb)

1.

My mother looks at me as I am no witness to myself
the summer before college, eighteen, when she states
in the mirror, that no man will ever love me
at this weight. The tears I don't cry
(then) mean I am not too weak
to receive such honesty.
Maybe she is more
right than we
dare to
see.

2.

Sky—
and what
about woman.
When I return after
years away, after months
of silence, Mom barely looks at me.
When I tell her I was raped, she can barely
whisper it was a good thing she didn't raise me in Nigeria.
I look to her. Want to douse her in my tear-shaped arms, fat, like
a heavy blanket: the weighted kind they make special, for folks who have trouble
looking you in the eye. Or being touched. But I don't. Touch her. Or ask her to explain.

3.
Mama I'm going to sit by the river,
& eat joloff from the pot.
Come with me.

PROVERB

You must cut your coat by your waist,
you preach, when you catch me
reaching for a dress outside my budget,
as if it were a *cookie*, which we all know

was my first word. Not *Mama*.
Even when we don't discuss
gastric bypass
we do.

You ask if I am afraid
of the knife and I chuckle,
for I have been long-groomed
for the blade. Anyway,

it is not for me to say
how brave   only
that I would peel back
the fresh scabs

like a potato skin,
drag the slotted blade
across the surface
from syllable to line

one at a time
West to East
then West again,
if it would urge you

to grease the pan.
What if the body

is just the throw-away?
The spotted frailty
that barely drapes:
the words

we are unable to say.
The left over love,
no longer appropriate
to plate.

MIRROR TALK
(for M.P.)

the woman who faked cancer
was the first

                                 to reap the secrets
                                     of your body

her knowing hands
firmly turned

                                       your flesh
                                   into an orchard

every way one can lie
in beauty and truth

                                 she studied, or stole
                                     till the soil

dried yellow &
the stems hollowed

                            this season's empty harvest
                               moon: the single plate

before you
left her

                                   you forgave
                              her hollering *fat fuck*

the night she left you
in the car to swallow pills

                             your bottom barely fit
                  into the chair beside her hospital bed

she never said sorry
or meant it

                                  when she cried
                               all the fruit dried

& the days got shorter
& you got fatter

with brokenness
fatter with predators

your thighs
expanding into the night

FRUIT FLIES
for M.P.

At the top
of the list of things
we never talked about.

Could never talk about
at the top
of your list.

Is the baby
was
the baby.

How long did we keep him?
1 day?
Was it 3?

The life
of the average fruit fly
spans s e v e n:

7 days
in average conditions.
In optimal climates,

could be forty.
Might reach fifty.
Definitely.

Not.
3.

Before you found me,
how many days
of wanting.

Did you whittle
down
to 3?

I watched you
carry him back
through the same

                                                            doors
                                              as 3 days before
                                                           today,

without a say.
In Nigeria
seven days

                                        is when they gather
                                           around the baby,
                                          give him a name.

But Madeline,
you and I
know the truth.

                                              About the lives
                                                          that
                                                       perish.

Inless
thanoptimal
conditions.

THE GOOD NEWS

Because I believe you cannot stop a thing from existing
even if you kill it
is how I loved you

Because in my thickest vibrato, I sing for Sarah
even though she cannot hear me
is how I loved you

Because I crouch under the tilted sky,
even as these knees choke on their age
is how I loved you

Because rain melts the February snow, renders the sun redundant
even if it's just because I say so
is how I loved you

Because my tongue points true north
even with this mouth of ghosts and hard swallows
is how I loved you

Because   is how I loved you
Even   is how I loved you
is how

NOTES FROM LA CASITA

for Amiri Baraka, Bob Dylan, and Terrance Hayes

. . . and they were too busy singing
couldn't hear their own beauty
as they were tuning it

I was ringing 'cause
they were tuning me
still singing   and they were wearing

sweatshirts, fur boots
and the girl had flowers on her dress
but couldn't see them blowing in the wind

as she was singing, her eyes closed
and Amiri Baraka sitting on my right
drinking (what smells like) beer?

and when did the Alaskans start dancing
and throat singing like blacks
from the joints. Now Baraka is laughing

(still drinking) and the flowers are blowing above
her knees. I could be in Tuva or wherever

but I'm front row
at New York
Lincoln Center

still floating in the Terrence Hayes of *Blue Baraka*
(and he got up to leave as quietly as he came)

and I clapped without knowing it and my mind
changed (without knowing it) and it's been six years
since I gave my life away without knowing it

and the *tune* changed. Before I knew it, Baraka
was back again (I felt *Black Again*) the music

hymning through our bodies, maybe God's
instruments, brought me back to where
I had stopped writing and begun

to revise.

AFTER THE FEAST
after Sir Derek Walcott

We cackle 'round the table
as my mother pries the marrow
from the bone. She has technique
—uses her fingers to find the weakness

where the circumference narrows,
then *crack*. It is remarkable
to hear her ivories unlock
dark gold, watch her tongue tunnel

out that prized meat.
Now, I am thirty
and mommy is careful not use the word *breakup*,
instead:

she might pull at
the shirt to cover my backside,
inquire about my plans
for the day,

suggest I go
to the gym.
Insist
she'd warned me

no one could love me
at this weight.
Mum still finds benediction
in the teeth.

Childhood is the best time for a clean break.

Spill   off the slide
tumble   down the stairs.
They say   when you crack
a mirror you're promised

seven years of bad luck:
makes no difference
if you split it in two
in four

in finity.
The angles can't confide
their secrets. But early one morning,
after the bone's been sundered,

the memoir unmarrowed,
ghosts swallowed,
you will suck
your teeth

and wake
to the splinters
on your tongue, searching the corners
of your lips for small morsels.

ALLĀHU AKBAR:
FOR MY BODY
UNDER THE RULE
OF WHITE SUPREMACY

Go ahead &   cry
Go ahead &

                  tweet

                  ignore

                  delete

                  devour

everything you can
fit onto your tongue

Go ahead   lie
Uncover or seekcover

Go ahead &   hold your breath
walking in brown skin

past a murder
of men

                        a flock
                        a congress

                        on the North Lawn
                        in the subway
                        outside mosque

at first light

                                        Just around

the bend   Go   ahead
Breatheunderwater
"

"

"

"

"

"

"

Lay down your words
D e s e g r e (gate)   your heart
Pick up   Lucille Clifton
Recall   the language you live in
Part   your six winged seraphim
Call   them to sing

on your knees

on your back

on your feet

Go
where the love is
The Greatest

ACKNOWLEDGMENTS

Poems in this collection have appeared in the following publications:

Online

"A Wall," *Thin Noon*, Fall 2017

"Call to prayer: for my body under the rule of white supremacy," *Crab Fat Magazine*, QTPOC issue, February 2017

"GenderMotherFucker," *Luna Luna Magazine*, Fall 2017

"Haircut," *Winter Tangerine* Winter, WT2 issue, January 2017

"Mama Wata (I Should Have Known)," *Luna Luna Magazine*, Fall 2017

"Notes on la Casita," *Crab Fat Magazine*, QTPOC issue, February 2017

"Three Women / Two Transfers and a Token / One Reincarnation," *Cosmonauts Avenue*, May 2017

"Prologue to a Name," *The Recluse,* May 2017

"A Mother Can See More Sitting Down Than a Child Standing Up," *Public Pool*, August 2017

Print

"The Good News," *The Arkansas International*, Fall 2017

"Tides," *Newton Literary*, June 2017

"After the Feast," *American Chordata*, Fall 2017

Anthologies

"Fruit Flies," *Great Weather for Media Poetry Anthology*, August 2017

"Mirror Talk," *Black Lesbians: We Are the Revolution*, Sinister Wisdom, Winter 2018

"The Talk," *A Shadow Map: An Anthology of Sexual Assault*, CCM Press, January 2017